# SUB
# BUSTERS
## COUNTERING THE SUBMARINE THREAT

A P-3 Orion from Patrol Wing Ten, NAS Moffett Field California, slides down the glide slope to dear old runway *Three Two Right* after a 12-hour patrol over the Eastern Pacific

# Introduction

The battle between submarine and surface forces goes back, in practical terms, to World War 1, when German technology first confronted English tactical imagination. Then, and since, there seemed something unfair about the duel. The ocean is huge, a submarine is small and easily hidden, able to strike without warning against seemingly defenceless vessels and crews. The submarine has proved to be, with the aircraft carrier, one of the most effective weapons a nation may use for conflict resolution and crisis management. One of the things that makes the study of conflict interesting is the creative innovations that stress provokes. In World War 1, the convoy and the escort, along with depth charges and other innovations, ultimately helped counter and control the threat. In World War 2, the submarine again offered a nearly decisive threat, but through a fortunate combination of luck, imagination and innovation, the submarine was ultimately defeated. Inventions like sonar/asdic and radar, along with airborne ASW patrols and other techniques and technologies, were developed and applied to the Battle of the Atlantic. The German U-boat fleet, initially invulnerable, was ultimately defeated, going to the bottom with nearly all hands. Only a quarter of German submariners survived the war, their force suffering the highest casualty rate of the conflict.

Today, the submarine still prowls the vast oceans. Huge 'boomers' with nuclear power-plants and intercontinental missiles, small attack boats with 'smart' torpedoes, from dozens of nations, cruise beneath the waves awaiting the call to battle stations. From Chile, Iraq, Australia and the Soviet Union, from China, and Germany again, from Great Britain, and the United States, in big boats and small, are carried the missiles and torpedoes of the next fight, and it still seems like an uneven match, but today for different reasons. Despite the vast oceans, every submariner of every nation knows that there is no good place to hide from a competent ASW team. Despite the latest innovations in hull design, in powerplant technology, in the carefully crafted shapes and propellers, or in the use of artful tactics and strategies, every submariner knows that, when push comes to shove, life is short.

Anti-submarine warfare has become a military version of a fine art, an intricate and creative combination of technology and teamwork, of innovation and experience. The team includes ships like the sleek frigates and destroyers, with racks of homing torpedoes and magazines full of anti-submarine rockets. There is the great P-3 Orion, land-based strategically around the world, sweeping vast stretches of ocean on 12-hour patrol flights. From carrier decks the S-3 Viking departs to guard the battle group, sterilizing the seas for hundreds of miles. In darkness, in heavy seas, the Sea King and Seahawk helicopters take off from the tiny flight decks of escort vessels for close-in ASW missions. Not one of these planes or ships is a reliable defence by itself, but working in concert they are a team that makes a submariner's mission extremely dangerous. Here's how they do it.

**Right** Making the most of the generous ramp space available at NAS Cecil Field, this VS-32 'Maulers' maintainer has unfolded the wings and extended the MAD boom on 'his' S-3A. Attached to Air Wing One, VS-32 usually spend most of their time protecting USS *America* (CV-66), and her associated battle group, from 'enemy' nuclear attack submarines lurking in the North Atlantic and the Mediterranean (*Tony Holmes*)

# Contents

# The mighty wanderer

**Left** 'STARTING TWO!' Engine starts are a team effort, both in and out of the aeroplane. Inside, the Patrol Plane Commander (PPC) leads the cockpit crew through the 20-item *BEFORE START CHECK-LIST:* engines two and three will be cranked first, one and four while taxying. The lineman (a woman) watches for fuel leaks, fire, and parts falling out of the tailpipe since the crew's visibility is restricted. The PPC times the start and monitors the outside observer and the P2 (co-pilot) watches the gauges: temperature, RPM, pressures and flows. Although a lot of controls have to be properly configured, actual starting is simple and automatic: select the engine with the engine start selector switch, and push a button. The honours go not to the pilots, but the flight engineer. Pushing the button starts the start sequence: bleed air from a start cart flows into the engine, spinning the compressor stage. At 16 per cent of maximum start RPM fuel starts to flow, at 33 per cent it should light off, and the big turbofan starts to sing its song with a single soaring tone, rising in pitch. Fuel flow warning light OFF, OIL PRESS needle and rising in both sections, EVC lights out, FUEL PUMPS in parallel; between 57 per cent and 64 per cent the start button pops out, start light goes out. You're in businesss with Engine Two

**Below** It's a long way to the top if you want to fix a P-3. One mechanic and a gaggle of supervisors inspect the guts of an Orion's horizontal stabiliser

**Above** VP-19's fleet of airships are dwarfed by a hanger from another time. Moffett Field has hosted long range patrol aircraft since the 1930s, but back then it was a massive lighter-than-air dirigible housed in even more massive buildings like Hanger One. During World War 2 Moffett was home to ASW dirigibles, one of which was stabled in the hanger in the background

**Right** Here we go again. The training squadron's aircraft await the attentions of student crews whilst one of their number makes 'left traffic' for yet another touch-and-go

**Above** One crew from VP-19 after a challenging, dangerous, and difficult mission – supporting a photographer doing a book on ASW. The dangerous part occurred when they let him fly the aircraft

**Above right** The junior pilot gets the responsibility of lugging the Comm box and its secrets. Despite what the crew tells you, it doesn't contain the PPC's lunch. It is actually for the classified stuff required for modern bloodshed – codes for communications and weapons, battle plans, and a pastrami sandwich. Two locks secure it, the two pilots each carry keys for one

**Below right** Lt Skip Albee, Third Pilot (known affectionately as the 3P) on this crew, follows a respectful two paces astern of the PPC. The Comm Box is carried normally by the 3P, the junior pilot and newest member of the crew

**Above** LCDR Robert Madson, enroute to his semi-trusty steed. He is the big boss for today's mission, the Patrol Plane Commander or 'PPC'

**Right** The ominous looking magnetic anomaly detector, called the *MAD*. While it looks like a stinger, it is really just a sensor that is used to inspect the magnetic field beneath the aircraft. Submarines, particularly the older designs, create a magnetic 'signature' that is easily identified under the right conditions. The MAD is only one of the tools of the ASW trade, used along with radar, sonar, and the good old 'Mark One Eyeball' for detecting members of the loyal opposition

**Above** A brace of BDU 45s with Snakeye retarded iron bombs on the trolley, waiting for the ordnance crew to sling them on the racks. The fins pop open after release, slowing the weapon and allowing the Orion to make a quick getaway

**Above right** Another view of the BDU 45, as yet unfused, as it is carefully inspected by one of the ordnance crew. When fused with a four second delay Mk 15 fuse, the bomb may be used against a surfaced submarine. A near miss, while not necessarily fatal to the sub, will still prevent it from launching a missile or torpedo

**Below right** A Mk 65 mine is lashed firmly to one of the pylons. It rests on the bottom until a submarine or surface vessel's magnetic influence passes by

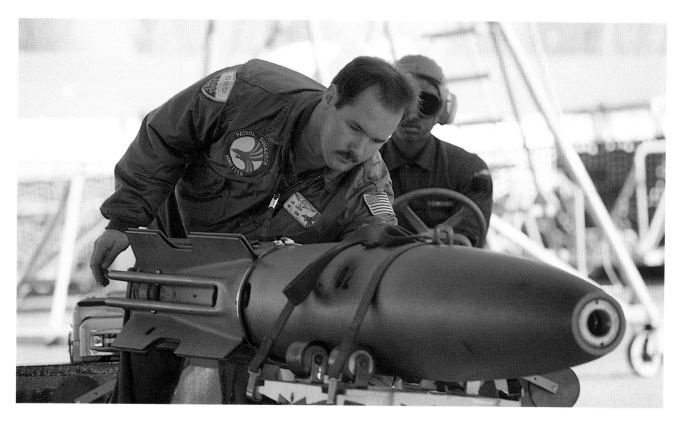

**Above left** A Mk 20 Rockeye cluster bomb offers the Orion a last-ditch opportunity to subdue a surfaced opponent. After release the Mk 20 spews dozens of bomblets which detonate at low altitude, creating tactical difficulties for a submarine or other adversary unfortunate enough to fall within its pattern of destruction

**Above right** Mk 65 mine. Fusing is the last step, and is always done *very* carefully and by the book

**Right** Once the weapon is slung on the pylon it must be rigged and secured correctly. Orion crews are easily embarrassed by such devices coming loose at inopportune moments

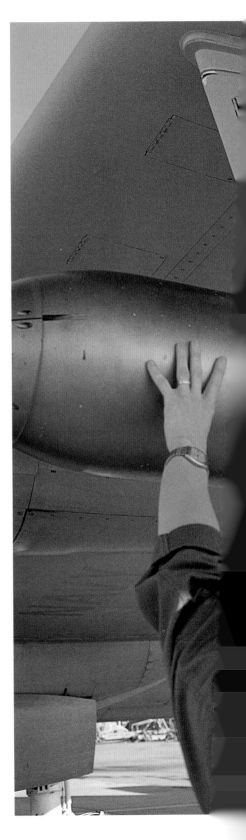

**Left** All decked out in the Navy's tactical grey paint scheme, one of VP-19's stable of Orions awaits orders. Until recently, all Navy aircraft were painted in a rather garish and tasteless combination of glossy hues, visible at long range. Since then, at great expense this new, elegant scheme has been selected. It goes *so* nicely with the cut flowers on the weapons systems operator's console

**Above** The Orion's tall vertical stabilizer

**Above** 'Starting three'

**Right** 'Pull forward!' signals the lineman. With engines two and three up and running, AFTER START CHECKLIST complete, and the permission of ground control, we're ready to taxy. Visibility for the crew is restricted so linemen help avoid the embarrassment of meshed wingtips by guiding the Orion as it waddles out of the nest

**Right** 'Left turn' is the signal, and the aircraft is now cleared to the taxyway. Ground steering on the P-3, like most large aircraft, is done with a little steering wheel linked to the nose gear. The system is sensitive, and pilots new to the Orion find themselves wandering down the taxyway in a drunken fashion until they get the hang of it

**Below** Number three engine; it's an Allison T56-14, and if you're in a hurry it can put out 4600 shaft horsepower

**Left** Take offs are, well, straightforward. Apply full power, use the rudder pedals to track the centerline, at 110 knots indicated airspeed the right seat pilot (watching the instruments) calls 'rotate', and the left seat pilot (who's driving) applies just a bit of back pressure on the control column. The nose lifts easily and the wheels leave the concrete. Then the great Orion slips the surly bonds of earth once again. As soon as a positive rate of climb is established, the P2 calls 'Gear up!' and we are out of here

**Above** VP-19 pilots, and all the other Orion drivers from Patrol Wing Ten who call Moffett Field home, use a standard instrument departure pattern called WOODSIDE 9 to safely escape the crowded traffic over the San Francisco Bay area: runway heading to 1700 feet AGL (Above Ground Level), left turn to the Woodside VOR (radio frequency), then climb to 3400 and a heading of 270 degrees until out of the TCE (Terminal Control Area) and over the Pacific

**Left** The Orion has a huge cockpit, unlike most military tactical aircraft. That's just as well, because when the mission lasts 12 hours, you need some room to manoeuvre inside the plane

**Above** Lt Vic Engle drives the bus. Enroute to the patrol area, up at altitude, there's not much to get excited about. The hard part comes later, when our hero takes this big beast down to the wavetops, skimming along just over the surface at 200 knots in search of prey. The circular device in the middle of the panel is a multifunction display, used for navigation and tactical manoeuvring. It shows data provided by the Tactical Co-ordinator and the Navigator/Communicator, both back in the 'tube', and is quite handy for keeping track of where you and the opposing team are located

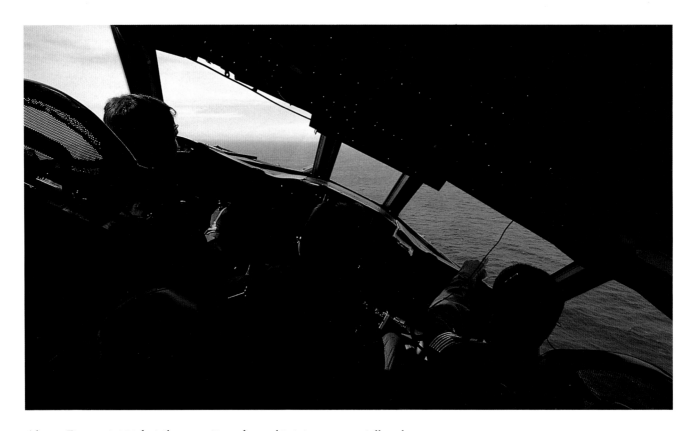

**Above** Down at 200 feet the sensation of speed is intense, especially when you roll into a turn. Lt Engle honks the P-3 over, coming right to 173 degrees at the beginning of a search pattern

**Above right** Back in tourist class, Lt Skip Albee, the Navigator/Communicator, does his best to keep his associates up front from becoming *totally* lost. The NAV/COMM uses inertial navigation systems to keep track of the aircraft's current and relative position since normal radio navigation aids aren't available at low altitude offshore. He also maintains radio contact with the outside world while the pilots stay busy keeping the Orion aloft and tactically useful. This is the entry level position for officer members of the P-3 crew, after which they move up and over to the Tactical Co-ordinator's seat across the aisle

**Below right** 'Stand by for port side rig – ten seconds.' One of the Orion's major missions involves intelligence gathering for later use, and that's what this big camera is used for. It uses 70 mm film and a motor drive that permits highly detailed photography of contacts on the surface, a process called 'rigging'. This normally involves flying alongside a ship about 200 metres to starboard while somebody blasts away with the camera. Later, back at the ranch, the film is processed and studied by the 'intel weenies' at the 'puzzle palace'

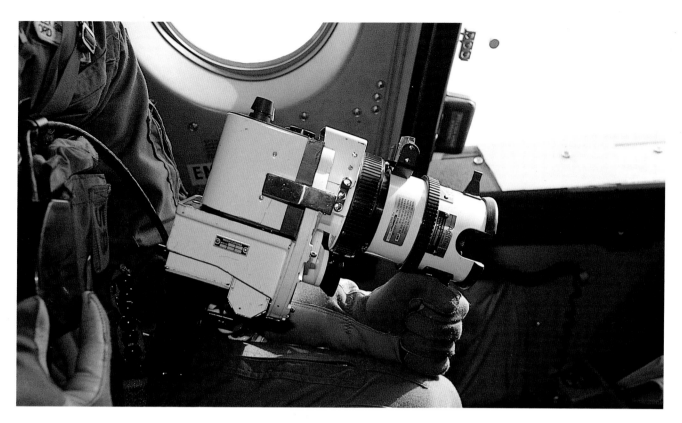

**Above** A Mk 77 sonobuoy is loaded into the 'P' chute. The sonobuoys come in many varieties, active and passive, but all serve the same basic function. They listen to the sounds of the sea, and send them back by radio to the Orion for careful consideration. One buoy in the water alone isn't much use, but with two or three the P-3 sensor operators can see a contact, watch it move, and tell if it's a whale or a sub

**Right** The 'TACCO' station is just aft of the cockpit on the port side, forward. Here's where the Tactical Co-ordinator works his magic, bringing all the information from the MAD, radar, sonar, and the 'Mark One Eyeball' together. The TACCO is the power behind the throne, selecting contacts and offering them to the pilots through the display on the instrumental panel

**Above** Lt 'Skip' Albee, the P3, constantly plots and schemes at his station, just aft of the cockpit on the right side of the aircraft. He keeps track of where buoys are dropped, of the aircraft's current position, and backs up the inertial navigation system (which drifts) with frequent sun and star shots using a sextant

**Right** The sensor operator's station amidships is really the heart of the P-3, where the all-seeing, all-knowing staff eavesdrop on all creatures great and small beneath the surface. They work with the TACCO to design buoy patterns that will provide the data required to locate, identify and – if necessary – kill subs. An old SENSO can tell from his data *which* sub – and sometimes *which* whale

**Above** 'Gear down and locked, 500 feet. You're reviewed and complete –
cleared to land' is the call as the old Orion slides back down to Moffett Field's
Two Nine Left

**Right** Many, many miles from its home base at NAS Brunswick in Maine, a
nondescript P-3C from Patrol Wing Five closes on the main strip at RAF
Brawdy after a trans-Atlantic flight from Reykjavik, Iceland. Regularly spotted
at west coast RAF bases throughout the year, Navy P-3s often stop over for a
night of hospitality with their maritime patrol counterparts in the RAF on their
way down to, or back from, NAF Sigonella, Italy (*John Dibbs*)

**Above** Specially spruced up for its participation in the 1990 Battle of Britain Airshow held at Boscombe Down in Hampshire, this VP-68 'Blackhawks' P-3B looks as fresh as any low-viz Orion can. A veteran with over 20 years of maritime patrolling to its credit, BuNo 153431 calls NAF Washington, Maryland, home, the aircraft, and its controlling squadron, being assigned to Commander Reserve Patrol Wing Atlantic. Eventually, VP-68 will receive early P-3Cs as the frontline squadrons trade up to newer airframes. No less than eight VP squadrons make up the reserve patrol wing Atlantic (*Tony Holmes*)

**Right** The full-motion simulator is a great place to prepare for the last seconds of your life. In this box you can experience engine failures and fires, severe cross-wind landings, battle damage, and all sorts of other versions of aviation hell. There are two versions; one for tactical problems that permit attacks on submarines, and the flight simulator for practising flight skills

**Right** 'Hey, isn't somebody supposed to be flying?' That's San Francisco off to port, and Oakland, California's airport, dead ahead, 60 seconds from touchdown. The simulation may appear a bit coarse in a photograph, but the effect is very, very real

**Below** Inside the simulator, a friendly crew of operators work hard to ensure that disasters always strike at the least favourable moment, and that every discomfort and inconvenience is offered to their student guests. The programmers are, in fact, other pilots from the squadron who've been taught how to torment their mates. Everybody crashes, sooner or later, but they all stagger away, better pilots for the experience

# The inner zone

**Left** The Landing Signal Enlistedman (LSE) reports 'deck clear for take-off.' A tried and true Sikorsky SH-3H Sea King from HS-85 pulls pitch from the deck of the carrier USS *Nimitz* (CVN-68) far out in the Pacific. The SH-3 has been with the fleet for 30 years of faithful service, performing close-in ASW, plane-guard, rescue and a multitude of other missions (*Joe Martinez*)

**Below** Preflight inspection. It's always a good idea to make sure the hoses are all hooked up, the linkages have all their bolts and nuts, and that nobody has left any tools lying around

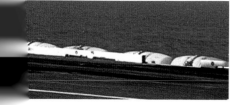

**Left** 'Hmm, I wonder what this thing is for?' Helicopters fly by virtue of an amazing multitude of components that rotate, flex, push, pull, or just vibrate, and it is in your best interest to ensure that they're all where they belong. LCDR Rob Leake checks the linkage of the rotor head, particularly the parts that let the blade unhinge

**Above** The SH-3 transmission is one component that you really want to work properly. Primary servos for the flight controls are in here too, along with the accessory section where all the pumps and generators are, with luck, firmly attached

**Above** 'Ready to start one. Spinning one!' LCDR Leake depresses the start switch button on the speed selector, beginning the automatic start sequence. The oil pressure comes up, the fuel boost pumps are engaged, and then the throttle goes forward to Ground Idle; at 20 per cent RPM the engine lights off and you watch the turbine internal temperature gauge as it spins upward, watching for a hot start – anything over 840°C. With number one alive and well it's time for number two – 'Ready to start two. Starting two!'

**Right** When the airframe is 30 years old, things get creaky. A last minute adjustment and check before a training mission

**Left** The LSE signals 'hold' to the pilots prior to rotor engagement

**Below** The LSE gives the crew permission to engage the rotors

**Right** With the taxy checklist now successfully completed, the SH-3 crew wind on the collective pitch and motor away from their hardstand towards the runway

**Right** Off the deck and safely airborne, the pilots sing the take-off checklist duet: 'Gear up? Power? Back to 100 per cent, security check? Complete.' Then the pilot calls 'stand by automatic.' Hi-ho, hi-ho, it's off to work we go. The co-pilot sets up the doppler and the coupler for the kind of approach the pilot intends for his first dip. That's also the crewman's warning to get the sonar gear up to speed and ready, and when he's good to go, his call is 'Sonar kilo alpha!' (fully mission capable)

**Below** The massive hinges that permit tail folding aboard ship. The SH-3 is a big helicopter with an awkward shape, hard to stow neatly in a closet of any size, even one as big as a carrier's hanger deck. However, blade and tail folding help

**Left** On station, the SH-3 prepares to relieve another aircraft from the squadron and the crew needs to know what (if anything) has been happening. 'IZOD 612, I'm famished', is the call for information and request for an update. 'Roger 612, Pointer One Nine is hot. Proceed two four zero degrees 200 yards' is the response. Then, on station, we call the ship 'IZOD 612 on station, mark dip.' Then the pilot calls the sensor operators: 'On doppler', and then, 'Down dome!'

**Above** The sonar control panel. With the dome 400 feet below the surface, the crewman gets to eavesdrop on every aquatic secret. The sonar has both active (pinging) and inactive modes. Once you start pinging, every sub from here to the next ocean knows where you are and what you're doing, and takes immediate countermeasures.

**Right** Working a search is done by quadrants, looking for large needles in a global haystack. It is an art form that takes years of training, experience, and coaching

**Above** Is it a whale or a 'boomer?' Two crewmen usually work the console, one doing the actual search, the other working the plotter, watching the hard copy for subtle changes in the sounds of the sea

**Left** AW2 Barry Stults, one of the essential crew that make the SH-3 a valuable, mission capable platform. The enlisted crewmen are trained in several skills, and most are qualified swimmers, prepared to assist with the rescue of pilots who have missed the carrier and landed in the water

**Above** 'IZOD 612,' the carrier calls, 'we've got an ejection, one five two degrees, 27 miles. Your signal is BUSTER.' That's aircraft carrier language meaning 'We've got a pilot in the water, you hurry up and go get him.' 'Up dome!' is the pilot's immediate call on the ICS, the ASW mission postponed for a while. Then: 'Rig for rescue!' While the pilots wind the old Sea King up to its full 120 knots (and maybe beyond), and everything shakes so much you can't read the gauges, the crew prepares. When the swimmer is suited up and all is ready, they call 'Rigged for rescue!' Once over the victim, the hoist operator flies his craft with a small joystick by the door, sliding the helo over until the sling is in position for the hoist

**Left** The 'eyes' of the SH-3H, stowed in its housing. The AQS-13E dipping sonar, built by Bendix, has been an integral part of the Sea King helicopter since the US Navy's vast fleet of SH-3s was upgraded to 'Hotel' specs between 1972 and 1980 (116 converted)

**Right** The cable reel can rapidly drop or retrieve the dome to depths of 400 feet. The AQS-13 system was developed from the 1955-vintage AQS-10 dipping sonar, the newer kit having a wider sonar scan pattern with greater sensor capability

**Left** 'Dome wet. Sonar submerged light' is the call when the dome hits the water, exactly 40 feet beneath the helicopter. The dip cycle, from transducer (sonar) launch to recovery is two to three minutes

**Right** 'Down dome'. The 'active' sensor disappears below the surface to commence its' 'pinging' search pattern

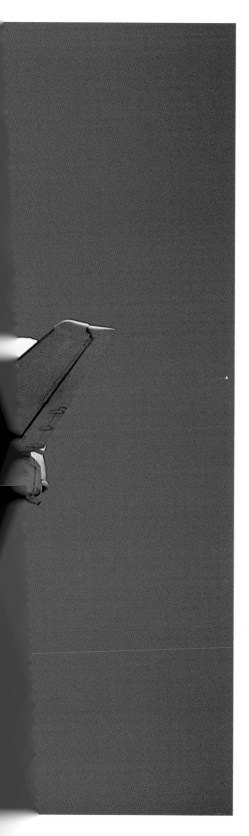

# 'Nordic' hunter

**Left** Arguably the most compact, yet effective, sub-hunter killer in service with the US Navy today is the Lockheed S-3 Viking. Unlike the P-3, the Viking was designed from scratch as a purpose-built ASW platform, its comparatively small size allowing it to grace a carrier deck in large numbers. Now a veteran of almost 20 years frontline service, the Viking is currently undergoing a mid-life update which will allow the portly Lockheed to 'turbofan' on into the 21st century. Back in February 1974 however, the operators of this drab S-3A were just receiving their first Vikings, VS-41 'Shamrocks' being charged with the responsibility of licking the aircraft, and more importantly its associated systems, into shape before the first S-3s went to sea. Although photographed in the 1980s whilst on approach to NAS North Island, this particular Viking was one of the first airframes accepted by the Navy from Lockheed's Burbank facility in California

**Above** The most heavily utilized Vikings in the Navy's inventory, VS-41's 15-strong fleet of S-3As and Bs pound the circuit at both NAS North Island and their 'satellite field', NAS Miramar, which is just up the road. Tasked with training raw pilots, Taccos and Sensos in the fine art of ASW, Viking-style, the 'Shamrocks' have developed a finely honed programme which sees a constant stream of new crews leaving the squadron after seven months of intensive flying, destined for frontline units. Coming in for another 'bump and burn' after completing an ASW sortie off the San Diego coast, this S-3 clearly exposes its 60-shot sonobuoy tube launcher area to the camera. Whereas the P-3 crew can reload the sonobuoy launchers from within the aircraft, the Viking Tacco and Senso cannot. This means that a wide range of passive and active buoys have to be loaded into the S-3's launcher tubes before the sortie commences

**Right**  Having completed their mission, the crew of '711' prepare to trap back aboard the carrier. With a 600-mile combat radius, the Viking is a highly desirable asset for any battlegroup commander, its surface search ability being heavily utilized during WestPac and Mediterranean cruises. Capable of tracking and classifying targets at great distances, the 'eyes' of the S-3 are hidden beneath its bulbous nose radome; a powerful Texas Instruments APS-116 high resolution radar specially designed for overwater operations. A drastically upgraded version of this radar, designated the APS-137, is being retrofitted to refurbished S-3Bs which are now entering frontline service. The new system differs from the '116 in having an Inverse Synthetic Aperture Radar (ISAR) which presents the crew with a two-dimensional, computer generated image of the target being tracked. The APS-137 is also compatible with the deadly AGM-84 Harpoon anti-ship missile (*Tony Holmes*)

**Below** 'Showtime'. GRIFFIN 711 rides the elevator up from the protected spaces of *Ranger's* hangar bay after having a minor avionics problem rectified. Once off the elevator the aircraft will be towed aft and prepared for its next sortie by VS-38 deck crew (*Tony Holmes*)

**Left** As with all American military aircraft, the S-3's cockpit dimensions are generous in the extreme, the pilot and co-pilot sitting comfortably up front behind a heavily tinted canopy. The small hinged flap agape on the canopy framing covers the aircraft's inflight refuelling probe. Parked alongside the island on USS *Ranger* (CV-61), this particular S-3 was one of ten Vikings embarked by VS-38 'Red Griffins' during the carrier's emergency WestPac in 1987 (*Tony Holmes*)

**Above** A 'Screwbird' with a few screws loose! Sealed up against the elements, a rather sad looking VS-33 'Screwbirds' Viking awaits vital parts (like a complete General Electric TF34 turbofan) to restore it to its former glory. Up until the early 1980s, the Viking community suffered from rather chronic spares shortages and general unreliability of certain systems within the aircraft. However, as part of the S-3A Readiness Improvement Program (RIP) instigated in the late 1970s, the Navy finally authorized sufficient funds to keep the 180-strong fleet airworthy without squadrons having to resort to cannibalization of frontline airframes. However, it appears the supply chain stopped before it reached VS-33's parts shop (*Tony Holmes*)

**Left** Every inch of the S-3's portly frame is packed with avionics, particularly down near the nose of the aircraft. As can be seen here, the pilot virtually sits on the forward avionics bay. This particular S-3 belongs to VS-33's CO, the 'O1' modex always being assigned to the 'bosses' aircraft (*Tony Holmes*)

**Above** Waiting for the sea mist to burn off, a row of 'Screwbirds' sit quietly on the North Island ramp. Part of CVW-9 since the late 1970s, VS-33 have recently participated in WestPac cruises embarked aboard USS *Nimitz* (CVN-68). A typical carrier deployment sees eight to ten aircraft and twelve complete four-man crews embark aboard ship for anywhere up to six months of solid blue water operations (*Tony Holmes*)

Although the VIP (Very Important Plane) treatment is usually reserved exclusively for the Commander Air Group's (CAG) 'barge', the CO's aircraft sometimes receives special attention also. This is definitely the case with VS-37 'Sawbucks', '701' acting as the perfect advertisement for the maintenance shop at the squadron. Part of CVW-14 and formerly assigned to USS *Constellation* (CV-64), VS-37 and the rest of '*Connie's*' air wing crossed decks to USS *Independence* (CV-62) in early 1990 when their former home headed east for a long term overhaul (*Tony Holmes*)

**Above** From one extreme to the other! VS-31 'Top Cats' had a long history of fine looking paint schemes stemming back to their estabishment with TBM-3 Avengers in the late 1940s. Carefully nurtured and refined over the ensuing 30 years, the scheme worn by VS-31 in its first decade with the Viking was both attractive and distinctive. However, with the advent of 'tactical' thinking, three decades of 'airframe art' went out the window and was replaced by this! Suffering a particularly bad case of 'resprayitis', this particular airframe was one of the last S-3s built and previously served with VS-28 'Gamblers'. The small squares in the rear fuselage are fold-out steps which give squadron maintainers access to the spine of the aircraft (*Tony Holmes*)

**Right** Although the overall design and assembly of the S-3 has been justly credited to Lockheed, several other companies contributed significantly to the success of the final product. For example, the huge hingeing slab fin was built by Vought, this famous company being responsible for the wings, landing gear and engine nacelles as well. The decidedly 'Nordic' badge on the towering fin of this aircraft denotes that this particular airframe belongs to the Force Warfare Aircraft Test Directorate, based at NAS Patuxent River, Maryland. Regular visitors to Cecil Field, the FORCE Vikings are responsible for the testing and evaluation of all new ASW equipment, and how these systems can be applied in a service environment. Both A- and B-model Vikings are assigned to FORCE, as well as various models of the P-3 Orion. Framed by the FORCE S-3 is a motley VS-27 'Seawolves' S-3A, its MAD boom having been deployed for routine maintenance (*Tony Holmes*)

When the time comes to leave the
carrier and deploy back ashore, the
external hardpoints on the S-3 can
come in very handy. Loaded with
personal items and the odd souvenir
or two from several successful port
calls in the Med, two VS-31 S-3s wait
for the Cecil Field line crews to come
and unhitch the huge outsize travel
tanks bolted on the stores pylons.
These tanks are usually seen fitted to
the five US-3A COD Vikings
attached to VRC-50 at NAS Cubi
Point, in the Philippines
(*Tony Holmes*)

Getting the final once-over before departing on a routine ASW sortie, this VS-32 S-3 still wears the old style glossy grey and white paint scheme. To help achieve a degree of commonality in carrier air wing ASW capabilities, all AirLant Viking squadrons have received the Bravo model S-3 before their west coast counterparts. The upgrading of the S-3A to Bravo standards is achieved through the application of the Weapons System Improvement Program (WSIP) kit, developed by Lockheed to a Naval Air Systems Command requirement. The kit includes a vastly upgraded acoustic data processor (UYS-1); advanced sonobuoy reference system (ARS-4); AQH-4 analogue tape recorder; the superb new APS-137 radar; an ALE-39 ECM system which gives the crew the option of using flares, chaff or built in electronic jammers; and an ALR-76 ESM system that provides improved threat warning capabilities over the older ALR-47 fitted to the original S-3A. The conversion of airframes is carried out by a Lockheed factory team at the rate of 24 aircraft, or four squadrons, per year, a total of 160 S-3As being approved for eventual upgrading (*Tony Holmes*)

# LAMPS III

**Right** A LAMPS Mk III SH-60 Seahawk slides back aboard the US Navy missile frigate *Crommelin* out in the Pacific after a routine ASW mission. LAMPS is short for Light Airborne Multi-purpose System. The SH-60, tricked out as a LAMPS III, offers the fleet longer range, faster speed, and a 'real-time' data link that extends the ASW mission over the horizon. The frigate doesn't 'own' the helicopter or its crew, but borrows them from a squadron ashore for temporary duty

**Above** Prior to flight, one of the pilots carefully works his way through the SH-60 preflight, part of which involves a close look at the trusty tail rotor system

**Above** A final check of the blade folding mechanism before approval for flight

**Left** Smile for the camera! This merry band of brothers is from HSL-47, based at NAS North Island, California. Pilots Chuck Norberg and Pat Fitzgerald do the honours forward, whilst sensor operator Paul Dash keeps shop aft

1. MAKE SETTING WITH FINGERS
2. TAPE IF RUPTURED
3. TAPE IF USED IN AIRCRAFT
   WITHOUT BACK UP TUBE

CHANNEL

**Above** Twenty-five sonobuoys can be carried, each of which is encoded for identification by the push of a button

**Left** Then the buoys are loaded into the racks and secured

**Above** Although everybody has a primary skill, most crewmen are cross trained in others as well in informal classes on the flight deck. Here a fireman (red shirt) is learning the signal for 'blade droop stops in position,' from one of his mates, a fuel handler. The helmets are called 'cranials' and the vests provide flotation in the event of the wearer taking a 'dip' over the side

**Right** The LAMPS III has a magnetic anomaly detector (MAD) as does the P-3 and S-3, but this one trails out on a long cable in flight. The MAD installed on the Seahawk is a Texas Instruments system, designated AN/ASQ-81 (V) 2

**Right** The helicopter will be out of sight for the next three hours or more, but in constant contact with the ship. Normal flight ops involve skimming the surface at high speed, trying to stay below the radar horizon of the opposing team. Then the crews enjoy making mock attacks on the ships, trying to manoeuvre into position for torpedo launch before being lashed by the fire control radar of the victim

**Below** USS *Crommelin* launches its Seahawk under unusually favourable conditions. At night, with a heavy sea running, launch and recovery are a strain for the helicopter and the ship

**Above** Paul Dash is the master of ceremonies aft where he launches and tracks sonobuoys, deploys the MAD and passes the information on to the front-seaters

**Right** Lt Marc Bothwell, all tricked out for a night flight. In addition to the helmet, he wears about 20 pounds of survival equipment, including signal flares, a radio, a flotation device and a bottle of oxygen to breathe while trying to escape a submerged helicopter

**Opposite** 'Buoy's away!' A pop of compressed air launches the buoy, and a small drag chute stabilizes it during its descent to the surface. After a few moments submerged, the buoy pops out of the waves; the water activates it, turns on its radio transmitter and sonar sensor and it lives out its brief, busy life

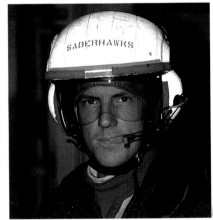

**Right** The sonar operator's display shows the relative position of the ship, the SH-60, the deployed buoys and the victim

**Above** The *Crommelin's* flag hoist and Sperry Mk 92 fire control radar. Developed from the Dutch Signaal M 28 system, the Mk 92 is a track-while-scan radar which controls both the Standard Missile (SM-1) launcher and the Mk 75 76 mm gun mounted on the frigate

**Right** The Combat Information Center (CIC) aboard *Crommelin*. The CIC is manned at all times and provides many services not related to combat. Here the movement of the ship is tracked, the radio monitored, the tactical situation – enemy and friendly – studied and displayed, and the battles fought

**Below** In this view of the CIC the 'air battle' console is clearly visible to the right of its operator

**Below** Out on patrol, HSL-47's Seahawk zips past another member of the surface ASW team

**Right** The elderly *Charles F Adams*-class destroyer, USS *Waddell*, (DD-24) still has a role to play in the ASW mission, even without its own helicopter capability. The LAMPS III gives the entire ASW screen a long-range, versatile and agile sensor, with over the horizon capability

**Left** 'Deck clear. Clear to land.' The Seahawk hovers momentarily before alighting on its 'perch'. The big 'pancake' on the underside houses the AS-4035 antenna, the 'eyes' of the powerful Texas Instruments AN/APS-12G search radar developed specially for the LAMPS III helicopter

**Above** Looking like the proverbial Christmas tree, the cockpit of the SH-60 is tactically lit so as not to interfere with the crews' night vision

Safety lights aglow, the SH-60 is readied for a night sortie in defence of the task force. Tradition dictates that should a submarine commander choose to attack a surface target, he will do so under the cover of darkness – hence the importance placed upon the LAMPS III's night capabilities

# Variations on the theme

**Left** Aptly named Nimrod after the 'mighty hunter' mentioned in the Book of Genesis, this sleek maritime patrol aircraft, developed from the de Havilland Comet 4C, has been the workhorse of the RAF's ASW force for over two decades. Strategically based in Cornwall and Scotland, the fleet of 34 aircraft are split between four frontline squadrons and a single operational conversion unit (OCU). This smart looking Nimrod MR.Mk 2P is being crewed on this sortie by members of No 201 Sqn, based at RAF Kinloss, Scotland. A famous unit with a very distinguished history, No 201 share a pool of 'unbadged' Nimrods with No 120 and No 206 Sqns (*Tony Holmes*)

**Below** From this angle the huge bomb-bay doors can be clearly seen. Capable of carrying depth charges, mines, torpedoes, Harpoon missiles or even cluster bombs, the Nimrod's unpressurized weapons bay is large enough to carry a healthy mix of weaponry to suit any occasion. Rubber bumper strips are attached to the bottom of both doors, and on several occasions these strips have helped minimize the damage inflicted on aircraft that have had to land with the doors agape owing to mechanical malfunction (*Tony Holmes*)

**Above** Although the RAF Nimrod force has been in service since the early seventies, not all the equipment jammed into the aircraft's slender fuselage is from that era. For example, this flight sergeant is operating the Loral 1017A electronic support measures (ESM) system, a sophisticated piece of kit built in the USA and only fitted to Nimrods in 1985. The system operator relies on the spiral helix receiver aerials within the wingtip pods to detect and display radar emissions from ships and submarines. Once a contact has been discovered he will attempt to match its radar footprint with others already stored in the system's memory. Equally at home tracking aircraft or surface radar contacts, the Loral system has drastically upgraded the capabilities of the Nimrod (*Tony Holmes*)

**Right** The Nimrod's 'front office' is functional, although not totally reflective of the latest in CRT technology! Slightly more cramped than the P-3's cockpit, the sharp end of the Nimrod was strongly influenced by the Comet, the two aircraft differing only in the former's more modern navigation and communications equipment. Photographed climbing away from RAF St Mawgan on an anti-shipping sortie, the crew of this Nimrod are attached to No 42 Sqn (*Tony Holmes*)

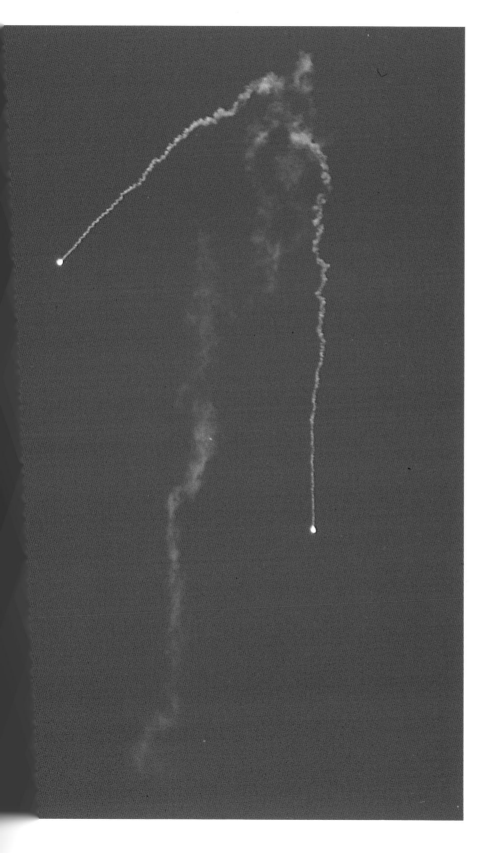

**Inset** When the Hawker Siddeley designers looked at converting the world's first jet airliner into an ASW platform, they decided that the best way of achieving the desired fuselage volume was to add an unpressurized 'bubble' beneath the existing airframe. The forward section houses the EMI Searchwater radar, whilst the majority of the remaining space is dedicated to weapons carriage, as can be seen here! (*John Dibbs*)

**Left** Over the past decade maritime patrol crews have started noticing the presence of navalized hand-held SAM-7 *Grail* anti-air missiles in the sails of many Soviet submarines. Designated the SA-N-5, the missile has given the submarine commander some chance of fighting back against his aerial foe, although most submariners would prefer to stay beneath the waves and retain the element of aquatic invisibility rather than slug it out in a missile fight on the surface. Nevertheless, Western maritime patrol squadrons have responded to this new threat by fitting various anti-missile devices to their aircraft, the most common being high intensity flares. Although the crews hope that they will never have to use them in combat, the flares do make a nice finishing touch to the Nimrod's airshow routine, this particular aircraft climbing away from RAF Mildenhall after completing its highly memorable display at the 1990 Air Fete (*John Dibbs*)

**Above** The Loral pods are clearly visible in this photograph. A passive system which gives out no emissions at all, the 1017A's high- and low-band aerials sit side by side at each end of the pod. All this capability does not come cheaply however, the price tag for the Loral system delaying their service introduction for several years. The large fairing inboard of the wingtip is the port external fuel tank, its equivalent on the starboard side having a 70 million candlepower searchlight faired into its nose. The wing tanks complement the internal fuel of the aircraft, the Nimrod's range of 9000 km being surpassed only by the Soviet Tupolev Tu-142 *Bear* in the maritime patrol world. This particular airframe (XV227) was one of the first Nimrods delivered to the RAF in 1969, the aircraft initially going on strength with the Maritime Operational Training Unit at St Mawgan (*Tony Holmes*)

**Right** With zero hour approaching, the co-pilot of 'Yankee Three Lima', alias Nimrod MR.Mk 2P XV248, checks over his route maps before preparing for engine spool up. A newly arrived pilot will spend up to 18 months in the right seat before earning his first officers' rating, thus putting him in charge of the 13-man Nimrod crew (*Tony Holmes*)

**Right** Common enemy, different shape. Both developed from airliners that enjoyed mixed fortunes in 'civvy street', the Orion and Nimrod have proven to be winning designs when it comes to maritime patrol, both types having now chalked up over 50 years of frontline service between them. Looking to the future, both the Americans and the British are going to be hard pressed to find a suitable replacement for these aircraft, particularly in the present climate of minimal defence budgets
(*Tony Holmes*)

**Inset** Proudly standing in front of 'his' aircraft, Flight Lieutenant Mark 'Seaside' Seymour has been with No 42 Sqn for over two years. Plane captain of Crew One, 'Seaside' was streamed on to the Nimrod after completing his flying training on single- and multi-engined types. No 42 Sqn shares 10 Nimrods with No 236 OCU (No 38 'Shadow' Sqn) at St Mawgan, the latter unit training all RAF maritime patrol personnel. As with their US Navy counterparts, RAF maritime patrol squadrons are somewhat on the large side when it comes to aircrew, over 130 pilots, navigators, taccos and sensos making up No 42 Sqn. The squadron divides its personnel into 13-man crews, each crew tending to stay together for long periods at a time to increase the overall effectiveness of the unit
(*Tony Holmes*)

With its 'brain' missing, this Nimrod rests in a rather forlorn state on jacks in the St Mawgan maintenance facility. Originally equipped with the dated ASV Mk 21 radar handed down from the Shackleton MR.Mk 3, the Nimrod force drastically upgraded its capabilities when the Searchwater was installed during the fleet's updating to MR.Mk 2 standards in the late 1970s. An excellent system that performs admirably over sea or land, the Searchwater excels at defining targets and reducing radar pulse clutter. Besides its installation in the Nimrod, the Searchwater is also carried by Royal Navy and Spanish Armada Sea King AEW helicopters (*Tony Holmes*)

**Above** All modern combat aircraft require regular maintenance to ensure that their complex weapons systems function properly. Because of the nature of their work, maritime patrol aircraft are perhaps the most labour intensive of any type in frontline service today, the combination of low-level flying, a salty environment and highly sensitive avionics resulting in airframes being grounded for long periods. Unfortunately, as each year rolls by the problems for ageing aircraft get worse, the Nimrod force beginning to show signs of extensive wing root corrosion. To combat these problems, the RAF has spent millions of pounds establishing extensive maintenance facilities at both Kinloss and St Mawgan to help keep the Nimrod fleet stay in as good a shape as possible (*Tony Holmes*)

**Overleaf** Bathed in early morning light, a freshly resprayed Nimrod MR.Mk 2P sits quietly on the RAF Benson ramp. A remarkably elegant aircraft, the overall shape of the 'mighty hunter' belies its aggressive role. The canoe-shaped fairing atop the fin originally housed the French-built Thomson-CSF ESM antenna, this system having originally been fitted in the Nimrod MR.Mk 1 from new. Now superceded by the superior Loral 1017A, the French system has been deleted and the glassfibre fairing filled with ballast to maintain the Nimrod's centre of gravity (*Robbie Shaw*)

Although not physically capable of tracking and processing sub-surface targets as quickly as the Nimrod, the Royal Navy's Sea King can deliver as hard a punch as any 'crab' (RAF) aircraft. Equipped with essentially the same signal processor as the Nimrod, the Sea King HAS.Mk 5 relies heavily on its AQS-902 Lightweight Acoustic Processing-and-Display System (LAPADS) to passively track targets using a mixture of sonobuoys and its internal MAD equipment. Masters of the art of ASW, the owners of these helicopters (No 820 Sqn) have been Sea King-equipped for over 20 years, the unit receiving their first Mk 1s in 1969. Seen here departing on a short exercise from HMS *Ark Royal*, the Sea Kings of No 820 provided ASW cover for the fleet during the Royal Navy's WestLant '90 cruise to North America. The helicopter in the foreground was the only Mk 5 on strength with the squadron at the time, the remaining seven airframes being Mk 6s (*Tony Holmes*)

**Above** Winding on the collective pitch, the pilot carefully clears the flightdeck of the '*Ark*' before pulling away from the carrier. Although basically a Sikorsky S-61, the anglicized Sea King differs markedly from its frontline 'brother' serving with the US Navy, its internal sensor fitment bearing no relation at all to the SH-3. Progressively modified over the years, the current frontline Sea King HAS.Mk 6 is perhaps the most potent of all current ASW helicopters, its AQS-902G-DS processor able to handle both sonobuoy and sonar data simultaneously. Digital electronics have also greatly enhanced the operability of the total package, and the installation of a CRT unit for the senso has allowed him to check the validity of his data before it is passed over to the observer's tactical plot (*Tony Holmes*)

**Right** Another country virtually surrounded by water is Canada, their maritime patrol force having to cope with tracking submarines in three oceans. Not possessing a carrier from which to fly ASW sorties, the Canadians have to rely upon individual Sea Kings based on frigates and destroyers, and the 18-strong fleet of CP-140 Auroras split between four patrol squadrons. Although numerically small when compared to the US Navy's P-3 fleet, the Auroras are perhaps the most capable Orions ever built, the Canadians specifying the installation of Viking avionics and data processing systems within their aircraft. Proudly flying the flag at Fincastle '89 (the premier ASW event for Commonwealth countries), this weathered CP-140 belongs to competition winners, No 415 'Swordfish' Sqn from CFB Greenwood, Nova Scotia (*Tony Holmes*)

**Left** Down amongst the swells is where the maritime patrol crewman earns his/her pay. On this occasion, the CP-140 crew are searching for a target beacon anchored in the Atlantic, some miles off the coast of Cornwall. Illustrated in this shot is one aspect of the P-3 family that has remained essentially unchanged right from the word go – the Allison T56 turboprop engine. A successful design so long associated with Lockheed military aircraft, the Allison engine has been steadily upgraded and refined over the decades, the power output of the T56 having increased accordingly. The four-engine configuration of the aircraft gives the crew an abundance of power to play with, the flight engineer often electing to feather a single engine (sometimes two) for long periods during the sortie to increase the aircraft's loiter time (*Tony Holmes*)

**Right** Although sitting in the right hand seat of a No 415 Sqn aircraft, the co-pilot proudly wears his No 405 Sqn crew patch on his sleeve. The cockpit layout of the CP-140 differs little from that fitted to the standard P-3 (*Tony Holmes*)

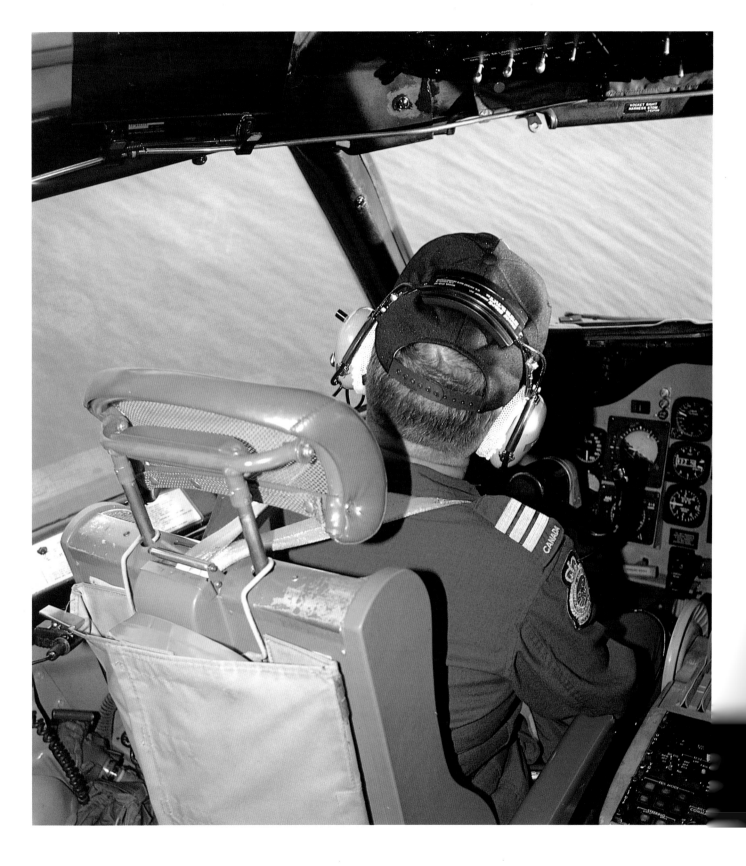

**Left** The visibility from the flightdeck has always been good in the P-3, plenty of glazing surrounding the left- and right-hand seats. On patrol for hours on end, the pilot and his deputy usually share the 'yoke time' evenly to retain a keen level of awareness (*Tony Holmes*)

**Right** The 'brain' of the CP-140. It is in this area where things begin to look a lot different from that encountered inside a typical US Navy P-3. The side-by-side seating of the 'wet' and 'dry' teams within the fuselage is unique to the Aurora, this style of layout obviously having its advantages because the proposed Orion successor, the stillborn Lockheed P-7, was to be fitted out along Canadian lines. Tweaking the AN/AYK-10 computer on this occasion is Sqn Ldr Andy Fryer, an RAF Nimrod tactical navigator on exchange with No 415 Sqn. Seated alongside him is Captain Harry Vincent, commander of the Fincastle winning 'champagne' Crew Six (*Tony Holmes*)

Sitting alongside the CP-140 on the rather soggy flightline at Boscombe Down was this elegant ASW hunter/killer from France, the Dassault-Breguet Atlantic Mk 1. Taking delivery of their first Atlantic in December 1965, the Aéronavale eventually received 40 airframes, 30 of which are still flying today with four flotilles. Armed with a Matra AS.37 Martel anti-radar missile beneath its port wing, this smart Atlantic Mk 1 belongs to 21 Flotille based at Nimes-Garon in Southern France. Along with 22 Flotille, the squadron are responsible for patrolling the western Mediterranean. Now slowly being replaced by new-build Atlantic Mk 2s, the old Mk 1s will, however, soldier on into the next century (*Tony Holmes*)

**Above** Defending champions at the 1989 Fincastle Trophy held at RAF St Mawgan, the Kiwis sent over a single aircraft to take on the 'best of the rest'. Staging through NAS Moffett Field, California, and CFB Greenwood, Nova Scotia, the Orion picked up several zaps from friendly line crews on its way (*Tony Holmes*)

**Left** Looking far smarter than its frontline compatriots, this pristine CP-140 belongs to the little known Maritime Proving and Evaluation Unit (MP&EU), based at CFB Greenwood. Perhaps best described as the Canadian equivalent of the US Navy's test and evaluation directorate at Pax River, the MP&EU perform sterling work improving the capabilities of the CP-140. Housed within the radome of this, and all 17 other CP-140s, is the AN/APS-126 radar, designed and built by Texas Instruments. A high-resolution, short-pulse system, the APS-126 is particularly adept at tracking submarine periscopes in rough water, or for high-altitude surveillance work, the radar sifting out extraneous clutter by using a fast-scan processor. This particular aircraft was making a rare overseas appearance at the 1990 Battle of Britain Airshow at Boscombe Down (*Tony Holmes*)

**Right** Over the past five years most P-3 operators from around the globe have drained their aircraft of any colour, the US Navy, for example, painting out the garish squadron markings that were once the trademark of their VP fleet. However, the diminutive island nation of New Zealand has ignored the low-viz trend and retained their small fleet of six P-3Ks in glorious full-colour markings. Assigned to No 5 Sqn, the Orions have performed sterling work for the RNZAF from their base at Whenuapai, Auckland, since the late 1960s. Originally constructed as P-3Bs for the US Navy, the Kiwi Orions have been extensively modernized in New Zealand during the late 1980s. New data handling and display systems, upgraded radar, infrared detection gear and Omega navigation equipment has all been retrofitted to the Orions, hence their designation change to P-3K (*Tony Holmes*)

**Overleaf** About to break into a 3g turn after completing a MAD pass over a marker buoy, Sqn Ldr Dick Newlands, crew captain of the No 5 Sqn team, firmly grips onto the yoke as the P-3 skims over the grey sea at a height of 200 feet. An experienced operator with over 20 years of flying under his 'lap strap', Dick Newlands has flown many types in his time with the RNZAF, including the Andover and the C-130 Hercules (*Tony Holmes*)